Stretch, and Twist

Collected by David Harmer
Illustrated by Wendy Sinclair

CollinsEducational
An imprint of HarperCollins Publishers

Contents

Touch

by Charles Thomson

Put your hands
up in the air.

Touch your feet.
Touch your hair.

Touch your knees.

Touch your nose.

Touch your tummy.
Touch your toes.

P.E.

by Ian Souter

In P.E.
we hop and drop,
and jump and bump.
We leap and creep,

and curve and swerve.

We reach up tall,
roll up like a ball,

then lie down flat,
on a mat.

And that's that.

I Can

by Tony Mitton

I can
be as light as a feather
or a falling leaf,
in windy weather.

I can reach up
really high
to touch the stars
in the great dark sky.

I can spread out
really wide
from side to side

or just curl up
and hide.

7

Cat Walk

by Robert Sparrow

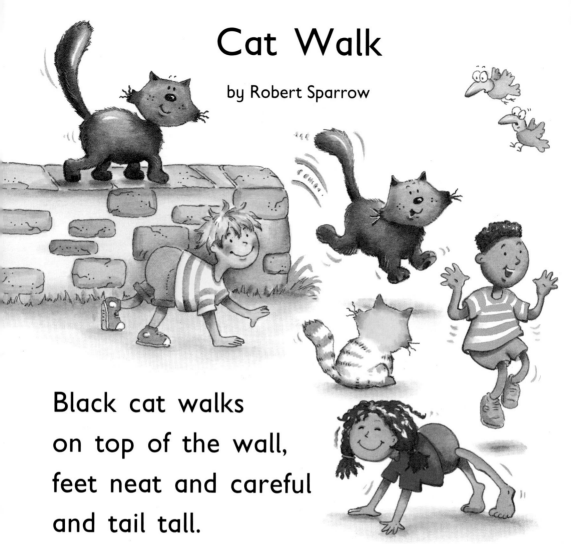

Black cat walks
on top of the wall,
feet neat and careful
and tail tall.

He jumps down
to the ground below,
stretches his body
long and slow.

He leaps to catch
a butterfly,
Claws stretched out,
Paws up high.

Then he sits down
and washes his face,
and curls up to sleep
in a quiet place.

Feet

by John Foster

Feet are for kicking
in leaves and snow.
Feet are for marching,
to and fro.

Feet are for running
up and downhill.
Feet are for standing on,
perfectly still.

Feet are for dancing and
feet are for skipping.

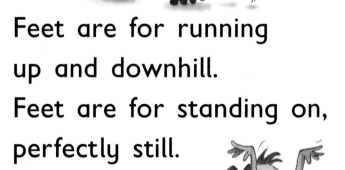

Feet are for hopping,
and sometimes for slipping.

Feet are for splashing
in puddles and rain,

and feet are for jumping
again and

again.

Stretch, Curl and Twist

By Trevor Harvey

I s-t-r-e-t-c-h my way along a bench
as sleek as any cat.

Then I curl into a hedgehog ball
and roll across the mat.

I twist like golden leaves that flutter
gently from a tree.

Then I spoil it all by wobbling
as I balance on one knee.

Storm Dance

By Ian Souter

The rain drops
plop,
then tumble
from a grumble
of sky.

The wind swirls
and whirls
around skeleton trees.

The lightning
clashes,
and flashes
across the sky,

14

while the storm
thunders,
and blunders,

sweeping its cloak of rain,
across the rattling window pane.

15